# Mulan

Written by Michaela Morgan
Illustrated by Steve Dorado

Long ago and far away, in a land of dragons and battles, there lived a famous warrior. This is the tale of that hero.

**OXFORD**
UNIVERSITY PRESS

# Chapter 1

 Mulan was working quietly in her corner of the house, just as she did every day. She was at her loom, weaving, weaving. Just as she did every day.

*Shhhhh, shhhhh* went the shuttles of her loom.

It was quiet in the house.

Mulan's father, tired and ill, was tossing and turning in his bed. Mulan's mother, busy as ever, was making a meal. Little Brother was playing as quietly as Little Brother could.

*Shhhhh, shhhhh* went the shuttles of the loom. But there was another sound. What was it?

It was the sound of Mulan sighing as she worked.

"What is it?" Father asked her.

"Why do you sigh?" Mother asked her.

"Are you dreaming of a boyfriend? Are you wishing for new shoes?" Little Brother asked her. He was a cheeky boy and liked to tease his older sister.

"I am thinking of the poster I saw in town," said Mulan. She sighed again. "Our country is under attack! We have been ordered to send a man from this family to fight in the Emperor's army."

WAR!
One man from every family MUST join the army to fight for the Emperor!

# Chapter 2

 "A man from our family must go to fight or we will all be punished," sighed Mulan's father. "I will do what has to be done."

The sick old man tried to struggle to his feet, but he had not even the strength to stand.

"You will not last a day!" cried Mulan's mother. "Your fighting days are over."

"I will go instead of Father!" said Little Brother. He picked up his tiny wooden sword and pretended to fight his toys. But he whirled his toy sword so quickly that he lost his footing and fell down. Oof!

Mulan looked at her little brother lying in his pile of toys. He was still clutching his toy sword. He was much, much too young to fight for his country.

She looked at her father. He was much, much too old. True, he had once been a very skilled soldier, but those days were long gone.

"I am just the right age," she thought. "I can run and ride better than many boys. I can think quickly and I have helped Father practise his fighting skills for years. I should be the one who joins the army."

# Chapter 3

 Mulan spoke up bravely, "I want to buy a saddle and horse. I will go to the army in Father's place."

How Little Brother laughed! "Silly, silly, silly!" he said. "You're only a soppy girl."

How Mulan's mother fretted, "No, no, no, it's not right. Your place is here with us. Girls are not allowed in the Emperor's army."

Her father was too tired and sick to say much. He just groaned, "No, Mulan, nooo!"

Mulan was determined.

"I have a plan," she said. "I will dress like a boy. I'll wear padding and armour. They'll never know I'm a girl!"

"Impossible!" said her mother.

"Dangerous!" gasped her father.

"Crazy!" said Little Brother.

Mulan had made up her mind. She was ready to do anything to save her family.

In the East Market she went to buy a speedy horse.

In the West Market she got
a saddle.

In the North Market she got
a full set of armour.

In the South Market she got
a sword.

# Chapter 4

At home, she tied up her hair and tried on her armour. All that night she practised her fighting skills and took tips from her father. She no longer looked like Mulan. Now she looked like a soldier.

At dawn she said goodbye to her father and mother, she climbed on to the back of her speedy horse and rode away.

"She'll be back by teatime," laughed Little Brother.

Yet Mulan was not back by teatime that day or the next.

Mulan travelled for three days along the banks of the Yellow River. The ground was hard, the air was chill and the nights were dark and lonely.

She missed her family and many times she wished she could go home, but bravely she went on. At dusk on the third day, she arrived at the army camp at Black Mountain.

As Mulan approached the camp a guard appeared, blocking her way.

"Where are you going?" he challenged. Mulan shivered, but she said in a deep voice, "I am here to join the army as ordered."

The guard nodded. Surprised, Mulan passed quickly into the camp.

From that moment on, Mulan lived in fear of her fellow soldiers discovering she was a girl. Army life was tough and every day sights and sounds reminded her of home and her family.

The days were long.
The nights were longer.
The life was harder than hard.

# Chapter 5

Mulan didn't give up. She worked hard and she trained hard. She learned how to use a spear and how to carry a shield. She learned how to attack and defend and how to ride at the speed of the wind.

Soon it was time for the first battle.

Mulan's blood ran cold with dread and fear. Her knees shook. Her heart pounded, but she clutched her sword tightly and went into battle.

Oh, she was as brave as any soldier!
Oh, she was as quick as any runner!

And she was clever! She used her sword but she also used her brain. She outwitted her enemies.

She used her spear to leap over her attackers. She danced her way past clumsy attacks. She hid under her shield then jumped out to take her attackers by surprise.

She earned the respect of her fellow soldiers. They still had no idea she was a young girl.

They clapped her on her back and said. "What clever tricks you use!"

That was the first battle of many.

She became a fine warrior. She became a leader.

She survived one long year, two years, three years, four, five and six and seven and more.

For ten long years she survived.

She travelled far.
She rode through
great green forests.

She rode across hot
red deserts.
She rode up steep
and snowy mountains.

She rode one thousand, two
thousand, three thousand miles,
four, five thousand, six thousand,
seven and more.
She travelled ten
thousand miles.

She kept her hair tied up, she kept her courage strong and she kept her secret well. She became a famous officer and led her troops into many a successful battle.

But every night she dreamed of her home, her mother, her father and Little Brother. She wondered how they were.

# Chapter 6

Finally the war was won. The Emperor was pleased with Mulan.

"You have been brave and true," he said. "Ask for any reward and you can have it. Gold? Diamonds? Palaces?"

Mulan knew exactly what she wanted.

"I want a fast horse and I want my freedom!" she said. "I want to leave fighting behind and return to my family to live in peace."

Her wish was granted.

When Father and Mother heard the sound of horses' hooves they came out to look. They saw a fine officer riding towards them.

It was Mulan, followed by her troop of soldiers. She looked so splendid, riding her fine horse.

Little Brother ran out to welcome the soldiers and to cheer.

Mulan went into the house to her old rooms. She sat at her old table and she took off her armour.

She let her hair down. She washed the dust off.

She put on her dresses, long and flowing.

Then she went out of the door and greeted her troop
of soldiers.

"I am Mulan," she said.

Her comrades were all amazed.

"A girl!" they shouted "Not possible!"

It took a lot of explaining before they could believe it.

The soldiers were so amazed that they told Mulan's tale far and wide. The story of how a young girl became a warrior spread from person to person, it crossed mountains and oceans to many different countries.

In Mulan's land people still sing about her.

*It is hard to believe*
*that it could be so,*
*but now we have learned,*
*now we know*
*not to judge people by how they look.*
*You, too, can be a hero*
*and have your tale told*
*or put in a book.*

3

# Retell the story

## Once upon a time...

WAR!

The end.

# A Winter Wonderland

Written by Karen King

Illustrations by Mario Capaldi

By courtesy of Hallmark Cards UK

MADCAP

One winter's morning, Star tinkled loudly under Tom's bed.

'What is it, Star?' asked Tom, yawning sleepily. Then he noticed snowflakes glistening on his window. 'It's snowing!' he cried, jumping out of bed.

He ran over to the window and looked out. Everywhere was covered in crispy white snow. 'How lovely!' cried Tom. 'I must tell Ed!'

# Make a snowflake

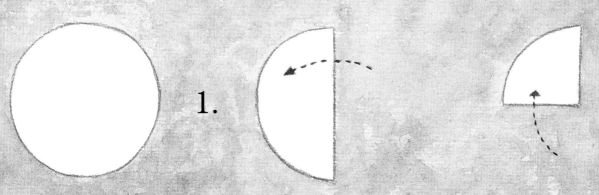

1. Draw around a cup on to white paper to make a circle. Cut it out.
   Then fold the circle in half, then into half again.

**2.**

2. Cut notches in the folded
   piece of paper.

**3.**

3. Open up your snowflake and hang it on your
   Christmas tree or stick it on your window.

'Wake up, Ed! It's snowing!' Tom shouted as he ran past Ed's room.

Then he pulled on his coat, scarf, hat and boots and ran outside. Splat! A snowball hit him on the chest.

'Got you,' laughed Kit Vole. He and Nonny Frog were having a snowball fight.

'Take that!' laughed Tom, throwing a snowball back at Kit just as Ed stepped outside.

Splat! The snowball hit Ed on the nose!

Good shot Tom!

How many snowballs
can you count
in the picture?

'Sorry, Ed!' laughed Tom. 'That was meant for Kit!' Ed decided to join in the snowball fight, too. He bent down to scoop up some snow to make a snowball but he slipped.

'Urrggh!' spluttered Ed as he fell headfirst in the snow.

'Oh, Ed, you are clumsy!' his friends laughed.

Can you spot the four differences in the two pictures?

After the snowball fight, Ed and his friends built a big
snowman. They rolled a huge ball of snow for its body
and a smaller ball for its head. It was quite hard work
putting the snowman's head on the body.

'Phew! Finished!' panted Tom. 'Now we need a hat
and scarf.'

'And a carrot for its nose,' said Sam.

'And two big buttons for its eyes,' said Nonny.

To make your own
snowman, you will need:
A cardboard tube, cotton
wool, coloured paper (cut
into circles), scissors
and glue.

2. Roll a ball of cotton wool to
make a head, glue it to the
top of the tube.

**1.**

**2.**

**3.**

1. Glue the outside of the tube
and wrap a layer of cotton wool
around it.

3. Glue on the paper circles as eyes,
nose, mouth and buttons. Why not
also cut out a scarf to keep him warm!

They fetched a hat, scarf, carrot and buttons and put them on the snowman.

'Hey, that looks good,' Edwina Hedgehog said as she came past. 'But there's something missing.'

She hurried off and returned a few minutes later with a flower and a shawl. She put the flower in the hat and the shawl around the snowman. 'That's better,' she smiled. 'Now it's a snowlady!'

  Can you spot these items in the picture?

| 6 | 7 SLEDGE TO NUMBER 9 | 8 | 9 | 10 | 11 |

| 5 |
| 4 BUILD A SNOWMAN MISS A TURN |
| 3 |
| 2 |
| 1 START |

Here's a fun game to play with a friend. You will need a dice and different coloured counters for each player. The youngest starts and the players then take it in turns to throw the dice and move the number of spaces indicated. If you land on a 'message' square, you must do as it says. If you land on a snowball, you have a free turn. The first person to reach the finish square is the winner!

| 27 |
| 26 L SCA 2 |
| 25 |

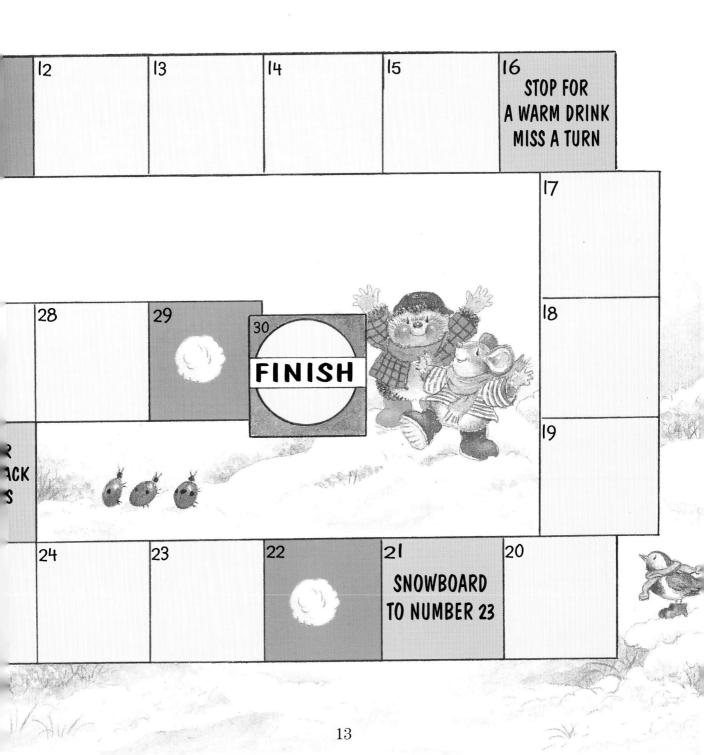

| 12 | 13 | 14 | 15 | 16 STOP FOR A WARM DRINK MISS A TURN |

| 17 |

| 28 | 29 | 30 FINISH | 18 |

| 19 |

| 24 | 23 | 22 | 21 SNOWBOARD TO NUMBER 23 | 20 |

Just then, Sam Rabbit came along. 'I'm organising a sledge race down the hill,' he said. 'Anyone interested in entering?'

'Yes!' They all shouted. Sam wrote their names down in his notebook.

'Right, be at the top of the hill with your sledges in half an hour,' he said.

# Make your own Country Companions

Trace around the figures and copy them
on to thin card. Then cut them out and
colour them in!

Now turn to page 21 to make a

winter scene for them to enjoy.

So, half an hour later, Ed and his friends all lined up at the top of the hill with their sledges.

Badger was the Umpire. 'Is everyone ready?' he asked.

'Hey, wait for me!' shouted Olly Owl, hurrying along with his new super deluxe sledge.

'Oh, no!' groaned Kit. 'We'll never win against that sledge!'

'Never mind,' said Tom. 'At least we'll have fun.'

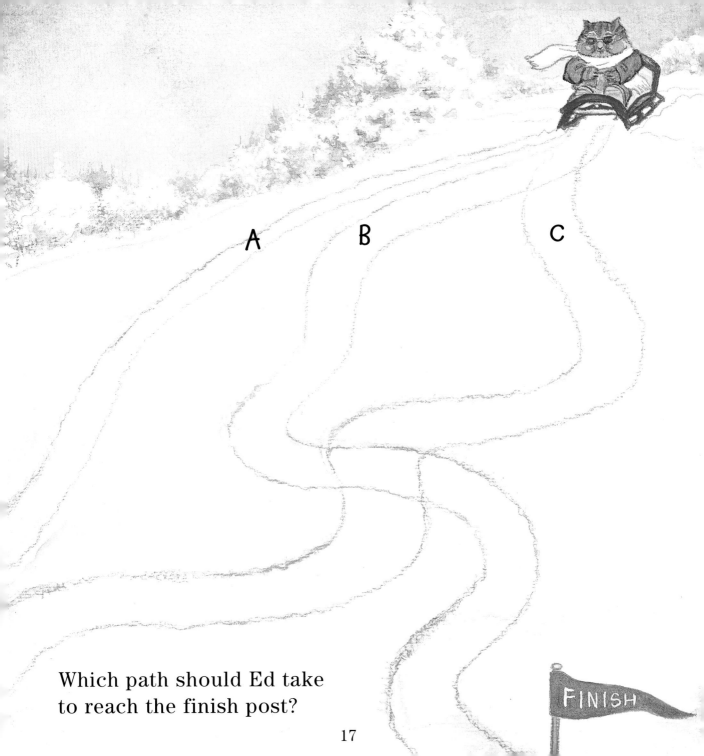

Which path should Ed take
to reach the finish post?

17

'Okay, everyone,' shouted Badger. 'Ready, steady, go!' The Country Companions all shot off down the hill on their sledges. Olly was soon in the lead.

'No one can beat me on this sledge!' he boasted.

But Olly was going too fast and he bumped into a log. His sledge spun around and Ed, who was behind him, crashed into it.

Can you spot the four silly mistakes
in the picture?

'Ooer!' gasped Ed as he fell off his sledge and tumbled down the hill, rolling over and over in the snow. 'I can't stop!' he shouted.

By the time he reached the bottom of the hill, Ed looked like a huge snowball!

'Hooray! Ed's won!' cheered Tom.

'Yes, but he was supposed to be racing on his sledge!' chuckled Sam.

**Make a winter wonderland** – First make a pond from silver foil and place it on a large tray. Cover the rest of the tray with cotton wool snow. Draw some houses on thin card, colour them in and cut them out. Stick them around the edges of your tray with paper clay. You can now act out your own Country Companions stories.

21

'What's the prize?' asked Mole. He'd heard all the noise and popped up to see what was going on.

'Oh dear, I forgot all about a prize,' said Sam. 'What would you like Ed?'

'A snack,' said Ed. 'I'm hungry after all that rolling in the snow!'

Everyone else was hungry too so they all went to Olivia's café and had hot buttered crumpets and warm blackcurrant juice.

'Now, that's what I call a prize!' smiled Ed.

How many crumpets can you
spot in this picture?

Answers to *A Winter Wonderland* puzzle pages:

Page 5   There are 10 snowballs in the picture.

Page 7   Spot the difference - the snowball is orange, the bottom of Ed's boot is green, two spots are missing from Nonny's shorts and Sam's scarf is yellow.

Page 17  If Ed chooses path B, he will reach the finish flag.

Page 19  There is a bird flying upside down, a flower with legs, a sledge with wheels and there's a fish in the snow.

Page 23  There is a crumpet on Ed's chair and one on Tom's, one on each of their plates, one on the plate on the other table, one on the base of the table and one on the hat rack.

---

Other titles in this series

**The Birthday Surprise** (read and colour)

**The Great Tidy Up**               **The Lost Wellingtons**
**The Photo Competition**               **The Picnic**
**The Summer Fayre**          **Tom Mouse's Disguise**

**The Summer Fayre** and **The Lost Wellingtons**
are also available as book and tape and as an audio tape
from MCI Children's Audio

First published in Great Britain in 1999 by Madcap Books, André Deutsch Ltd, 76 Dean Street, London, W1V 5HA
www.vci.co.uk

Text and illustrations copyright © 1999 Madcap Books
Country Companions™ © Hallmark Cards UK

A catalogue record for this title is available from the British Library

ISBN 0 233 99399 1

Printed in the UK